Colorado

WILDLIFE PORTFOLIO

photography and text by
LEE KLINE

FOREWORD BY CHRIS MADSON

To my parents, who encouraged me early on,
and to my granddaughters, Kailee and Genna,
who inspire me to continue now.

FRONT COVER: Thanks to the protection afforded by the Endangered Species Act and countless wildlife management professionals, the bald eagle, the enduring symbol of our nation, has made a strong comeback from perilously low population levels. Today, several hundred bald eagles winter in Colorado near large lakes and reservoirs and along major rivers on the eastern plains.

BACK COVER: His velvet crown nearly complete, this fine mule deer buck pauses in a patch of August wildflowers. In another month, the velvet membrane will peel off, unveiling antlers of hard bone to be used as necessary during the fall breeding season.

FRONT FLAP: With winter not far off, a yellow-bellied marmot gathers grass to line its den for a long hibernation nap.

TITLE PAGE: Regal, sturdy, and distinctive, the bighorn sheep is symbolic of Colorado and is the state animal. Bighorns are at home in rugged country, from low-elevation canyons to steeply tilted alpine ridges, where this group of bachelor rams is taking it easy.

BELOW: Pastel hues of a post-sundown sky delicately tint the water as a cow elk pauses while crossing the Colorado River. For wildlife photographers, putting cameras away before complete darkness sometimes leads to missed opportunities.

RIGHT: In the San Luis Valley, in other western valleys, and on the eastern plains, northbound flights of sandhill cranes in March and April are a harbinger of spring. Their almost prehistoric, croaking calls can be heard more than a mile away. The return migration from nesting areas in Canada foretells of approaching winter and usually occurs in late October.

ISBN 1-56037-356-3
Photography © 2005 by Lee Kline,
unless otherwise noted
© 2005 Farcountry Press

For more information about our books write Farcountry Press,
P.O. Box 5630, Helena, MT 59604;
call (800) 821-3874; or visit
www.farcountrypress.com.

Created, produced, and designed
in the United States.
Printed in Korea.

09 08 07 06 05 1 2 3 4 5

This alpine basin in Rocky Mountain National Park near Estes Park was most likely devoid of elk less than a century ago. When the Park was established in 1915, only twenty-five to thirty elk were known to exist within the boundaries. Today, the elk population in the Park is estimated at more than 3,500.

L ee showed up in the doorway of our magazine office without a sound, as he often does when he's on his way out for a shoot. I nodded to the empty chair and he sat.

"So whatcha been up to?" I asked.

"Pikas."

"Pikas?"

"Pikas."

I'm lucky to know a number of top wildlife photographers, so I've seen a lot of the harsh realities of the game at close range. One of the sternest is covered pretty well by that old epigram, "Time is money." Few people get into the business of photographing wildlife with that idea in mind, and even fewer survive without grasping it.

For a full-time freelancer, that means concentrating on the animals that sell. A lot of markets are interested in images of the charismatic megafauna, the heroic poses of trophy elk, deer, bighorn rams, mountain lions, bald eagles, and, of course, wolves that decorate everything in America from office calendars to the tails of commercial jets. A photographer who's interested in a continued supply of film, gas, and groceries spends a lot of time on this group.

Of course, this leaves another classification of wild things, which, for lack of a better term, I call the anonymous microfauna, the creatures that skitter and crawl in the background, unseen, unappreciated, quietly supporting the ecological weight of the world on their backs. Animals like the pocket gopher. The loggerhead shrike. Meadow voles. And pikas.

Lee was enthusiastic about the project. He'd staked out a talus slope at about 10,000 feet, sorted out the territories of the pikas in the rocks, and finally identified their favorite vantage points, their runways and foraging patterns. How long had he been at this, I wondered. Off and on for a month, he said, but he really thought the best shots were still in the future, right after first snow. I had a sudden image of him, hunkered down behind a snow-covered boulder with the north wind sweeping down off Trail Ridge like a scythe. I asked the obvious question:

"You figure on covering your retirement with pika pictures?"

He said he was hoping to interest *National Wildlife* in a photo essay. And there was always a chance of selling a calendar shot. And he thought he might even send a few to me. Then he smiled a little sheepishly.

"Okay, probably not," he admitted. "But they're really amazing little critters. I get a kick out of 'em. Another couple of months and I'll have the best pika file in North America."

That's Lee Kline.

The roots of Lee's fascination with wildlife and wild places undoubtedly lie in his upbringing. As a child, he prowled the foothills along Colorado's Front Range where the shortgrass prairie laps up against the Rockies. The landscape is a spectacular blend of horizontal and vertical, with every sort of wild place imaginable: the cottonwood bottoms along the Big Thompson, the river meandering through the timber, still cold and clean from the high country. The wetlands at the fringe of the plains catching the run-off from the mountains behind. The huge orange-barked ponderosa pines shading the first ridges, the black expanse

FOREWORD

by CHRIS MADSON

Editor, *Wyoming Wildlife* magazine

Try having a picnic in the Colorado mountains without one or more of these birds showing up! The gray jay, commonly known as "camp robber," is a year-round resident that is quite trusting—even pushy—around people with food.

of spruce and fir higher up, then the aspen groves, the twisted pines of the krumholtz, and finally alpine meadows and summer snow, all within thirty miles. This tapestry of habitats shelters one of the richest collections of wildlife on the continent. It is a corner of creation that leaves its mark on everything that grows here, including people.

In Lee's case, the mark was exceptionally deep. Like most of the real outdoorsmen I've known, he gets a kick out of any encounter he has with wild things. He's an ardent hunter and angler, but he's tickled to argue about the identity of a nondescript sparrow in the grass or a blossoming cushion plant in the high tundra. Like me, he has a taste for ridge-running—bushwhacking to the top of a distant ridgetop just to see what the world looks like from that unique vantage point. Considering his unquenchable interest in the outdoors, I guess it was inevitable that he would gravitate toward photography.

A nature photographer has to master an unusual set of skills. One has to be a bit of a techno-geek to grasp the operation and maintenance of today's advanced cameras and lenses. One has to read weather, know how to dress for it, and be aware of the unexpected challenges—and opportunities—it may offer. It helps if a person knows how to get a four-wheel-drive pick-up out of a mud hole, too.

ABOVE: Twin mountain goat kids rest up on a granite ledge before resuming their frolicking on some of the most dramatic and rugged terrain in the state.

FACING PAGE: After a morning of foraging, this black bear shuffled off into a nearby aspen grove for a nap. The bear was not too happy to discover it had company, but its intense stare was enough to restore its privacy by encouraging me to move on to other subjects.

One also has to understand the subject. With wildlife, that starts with identification and a basic grasp of natural history, but it doesn't end there. The best field guide in the world won't tell you where a big mule deer buck will bed down for the afternoon or which perch an eagle is likely to use when it's fishing. The best wildlife photographers develop an uncanny ability to find wild animals and anticipate their behavior, and Lee is one of the best.

Eventually, the pursuit of the perfect wildlife image leads some photographers to a special knowledge of wild places. Some of these become famous, like Alaska's McNeil River or Yellowstone's Hayden Valley. Many others are known only to the photographer who discovers them—the ridge in Rocky Mountain National Park where the ptarmigan spend the summer, the sagebrush rim in southwestern Wyoming where the pygmy cottontails hang out. They provide the backdrop for a great wildlife image—the color, vegetation, and landscape that set the ecological scene and establish the photographer's palette.

Ultimately, the best nature photographers learn to understand light. Ordinarily, they can't manipulate it the way a studio photographer so often does. They hunt natural light, waiting through bad weather, setting up before dawn, hiking miles, waiting for days to catch the perfect combinations of atmosphere and sun. When that combination occurs, it may last an hour or a second—the real professional has learned the hard way to be ready for the opportunity and take immediate advantage of it.

I've looked at thousands of Lee's images over the years, and I think he understands wildlife, wild places, and natural light as well as any photographer of his generation. But you don't have to rely on my opinion. The pages that follow are a distillation of more than forty years in the outdoors. Take a little time to look over Lee Kline's shoulder—see for yourself.

ABOVE: Often seen perched on utility poles or hover-hunting along roadsides, the American kestrel (sparrow hawk) is the most widely distributed and smallest of New World falcons. His first winter still ahead, this young male has chosen a favored hunting perch at the edge of a marsh.

LEFT: In mid-pounce, this red fox was so busy trying to catch mice that it seemed to hardly pay any attention to the camera or me. It soon became apparent, however, that the sly hunter was using me as a "beater" to help him locate unseen prey as it scurried away from my movements.

LEFT: Commonly mistaken for a chipmunk, the slightly larger golden-mantled ground squirrel is just as adorable and is found in colonies throughout much of Colorado's high country.

BELOW: On a blustery, cold December day, the tracks ending abruptly at the base of a snow-covered boulder had me perplexed. After several minutes of searching, I found this mountain cottontail in a cozy hide more than four feet off the ground. How it got there without disturbing one flake of the snow on the rock is still a mystery!

FACING PAGE: A few steps below 12,000 feet in elevation, a mule deer buck looks inquisitively at me. Mule deer are only found west of the Mississippi and were named for their large, mule-like ears.

LEFT: A western prairie rattlesnake suns itself on a ledge near the entrance to a suspected hibernation den near Brown's Park. On that October day, I found twelve other snakes within a few yards of this one, all catching some rays before the cold of the season pressed them into hibernation.

BELOW: The combination of thick frost, ground fog, and rich dawn light makes for a dramatic photograph, but the white-tailed buck completes the picture.

FACING PAGE: With short, powerful legs and strong claws on the front feet, badgers are built for digging. Opportunistic predators, badgers eat small burrowing animals such as ground squirrels, prairie dogs, and even snakes.

RIGHT: For most of a September day, I had limited success photographing this three-antlered bull elk and his harem. Sundown was ten minutes past when the bull and his harem appeared on the ridge. In the failing light, a sturdy tripod and cable shutter release helped to get the photograph.

BELOW: The largest member of the grouse family in North America, the sage grouse is found only where sagebrush is abundant. The white feathers on the breast of this male conceal inflatable air sacs, which are only visible during breeding displays and have the appearance of the old "Mae West" life preservers of WWII vintage.

ABOVE: A bull elk and his cow herd lounge in a secluded alpine basin well above timberline (and are hidden from other bulls, at least temporarily), providing a unique "aerial" perspective from high on the rim of the basin.

FACING PAGE: "What's that thing over there with one big, black eyeball?" might be what the pronghorn doe was thinking as she scrutinized my photo blind with a telephoto lens sticking out of it. The eyesight of pronghorns is legendary, and the animals can nearly see behind themselves without moving their heads (note their eyes are set outside the contours of the head).

FACING PAGE: In September, when fall colors are ablaze, so are the amorous thoughts of bull moose. Unlike elk, moose do not herd up during the breeding season. Instead, the bulls have to search out cows one at a time. Colorado's moose are of the Shiras subspecies.

RIGHT: Heavy frost and very cold spring temperatures probably have this roosted flock of yellow-headed blackbirds wishing they had stayed further south—at least until the morning sun warms things up.

BELOW: Just seeing a deer has always made me feel like things are right with the world. That feeling was doubled this September morning as two mule deer does wandered through heavy ground fog near Cumbres Pass.

RIGHT: A mature bull elk had thrashed this small pine tree earlier in the day. Whether instinct or mimicry motivated the bull elk calf, he, too, went a few rounds with what was left of the tree.

BELOW: A little high-country haymaker busily harvests food for the winter, one mouthful at a time. Pikas are gerbil-sized, year-round residents of talus and tundra slopes above timberline. They don't hibernate, and they spend the short alpine summers gathering, drying, and storing grass under the jumbled rock for their winter food supply.

FACING PAGE: Aspen groves, with standing dead trees, are good springtime locations for finding cavity-nesting birds such as the northern flicker. Both parents (this one is a male) work almost non-stop to feed the young until they fledge in mid- to late summer.

Many thousands of bull elk live in Colorado, but this Rocky Mountain National Park specimen had some of the most bizarre antlers I've ever seen. He had a sizeable harem of cows, but no other bulls made any attempt to challenge this unusually antlered herd master.

This coyote has located something to eat in the grass, probably a mountain vole. Coyotes are the personification of "survivor," having endured the persecution of humans visited upon all large predators during the settlement of the West. While wolves and grizzlies in Colorado disappeared under the pressure, coyotes endured and are found throughout the state, including within the suburbs of many metropolitan areas.

ABOVE: One of the more beautiful plovers, the killdeer is quite common around lakeshores and wetlands throughout the state. Their strident calls pierce the air when threatened or disturbed. It almost sounds like their name spoken with a "New Yawk" accent.

LEFT: Bighorn rams spend most of the year in bachelor groups away from the ewes and lambs. Long before the classic head-banging clashes of the rut, which usually occur between strangers on the breeding grounds in November, a dominance hierarchy or pecking order is established among rams in a group. The dominant ram in this bunch is walking aggressively and displaying his horns to the others to make sure they remember who's the boss.

ABOVE: Fall in the mountains and valleys rings with the eerie bugling of mature bull elk engaged in the annual rut. All that is truly wild and free is embodied in the melodic sounds, and to hear it is to be the richer for it.

RIGHT: Thousands upon thousands of snow geese use large reservoirs on the eastern plains as a rest stop during the winter migration. The cacophony of a large flock at dawn is hard to describe to those who have not experienced it.

Two red fox kits roughhouse at a spring den within sight of a major highway. Their play went on for almost an hour with one then the other gaining an upper hand.

LEFT: A drake blue-winged teal is a dapper fellow in breeding plumage. Generally, blue-wings are the last ducks to head north in the spring and the first ones south in the fall. Does that make them "fair weather" ducks?

BELOW: Spring green-up is the time many young animals make their first forays out of the birth dens. A young thirteen-lined ground squirrel, named so for the alternating dark and light lines on the head and back, forages on new spring grass in late April.

A herd of elk in Rocky Mountain National Park moves out
of the timber to feed as a December snowstorm intensifies.

Winter or summer, "home" to a mountain goat is some of the most inhospitable, exceedingly rugged terrain in the state, almost all of it nearly vertical and well above timberline.

RIGHT: That flash of brilliant blue, occasionally seen at the edges of summer mountain meadows or flickering through aspen stands, is most likely a male mountain bluebird diligently gathering morsels to feed youngsters in a nearby nest cavity. Bluebird males and less-colorful, grayish females are both doting parents.

BELOW: Porcupines are pretty amazing survivors. As the second largest rodent in Colorado, and the slowest afoot, porcupines should be easy prey for any number of predators—that is, until you remember the many thousands of barbed quills on their tails!

Shiras moose, the largest members of the Colorado deer family, were successfully reintroduced to the state in the late 1970s in North Park, near Walden. A subsequent release occurred near the Spring Creek Pass area at the headwaters of the Rio Grande River, as well as on Grand Mesa, east of Grand Junction.

RIGHT: Cougar, mountain lion, or puma—all are names for the same large feline predator. Rarely seen, they are secretive shadows of the mountains and river drainages of the state. PHOTO BY FRED EICHLER

BELOW: Heavy October frost covers a meadow and forms on the hair of a cow elk and her calf of the year. Although capable of surviving on its own, the calf will remain somewhat dependent on mom until the following spring.

Several long, cold March nights, spent listening and searching, went into capturing this moment on film. Quite tiny, silent except during breeding season, and almost totally nocturnal, the northern saw-whet owl is a challenge to photograph. This male has a "gift" for his mate.

RIGHT: When you have an itch, the only thing to do is scratch it, as this black-tailed jackrabbit is doing. Jackrabbits are not really rabbits; they're hares. The young are born covered in fur and with eyes open, and they're able to move about within hours.

BELOW: Also known as "antelope," the pronghorn is one of the most beautifully marked animals in North America. They are unique among horned animals in that they shed the black horn sheaths in winter and grow a new set by early summer.

ABOVE: If chipmunks, mice, and other small rodents have nightmares, the long-tailed weasel is most likely the cause. Found throughout the state, this slender, restless, and solely carnivorous hunter uses camouflage, cunning, and speed to capture prey. In winter, the weasel's fur turns white and gives rise to mistaken identity with the ermine. PHOTO BY CHASE SWIFT

FACING PAGE: In charge and proud of it, a herd bull displays his antlers for all to see during the fall breeding season. Elk cast (shed) their antlers annually, usually between the winter and spring solstices. Encased in velvet, new antler growth begins immediately thereafter and is complete by early August, just in time for fall nuptials.

ABOVE: A male broad-tailed hummingbird alights on a perch, but he won't stay there long. Its supercharged metabolism requires constant refueling. In flight, the wings of broadtail males create a unique buzzing or trilling sound that differentiates it from other humming-birds. PHOTO BY STEVE VAUGHAN

RIGHT: Summer is the time of plenty in the Colorado high country. These mule deer bucks in the Mummy Range are growing their antlers and putting on fat for the rigors of the fall rut and winter survival.

ABOVE: Spring is assured when the sights and songs of displaying male red-winged blackbirds fill the air around ponds, lakes, and marshes.

RIGHT: Nap time. After yawning, this mule deer buck bedded right where he stood and was asleep in minutes. The rut was on and apparently all the carousing he'd done for the past several days had finally caught up with him. Thirty minutes later, he was off again.

FACING PAGE: Appearing to be lazily enjoying a fall afternoon on the banks of the Big Thompson River, this large black bear has found a deer carcass nearby and is very reluctant to leave it.

ABOVE: November in mule deer country holds many surprises. Large bucks that remain unseen for much of the summer and fall lose their shyness when the breeding season gets underway.

FACING PAGE: Quit showing off and hold still for the picture! Young burrowing owls can be quite entertaining to observe and photograph. These small ground-dwelling owls are active during the day and relatively easy to find if present in an area. Adult owls make use of abandoned prairie dog burrows and dens of other burrowing animals to raise their families. PHOTO BY CHASE SWIFT

ABOVE: A year-round resident of the state, the northern harrier (marsh hawk) is a common sight gliding along fencerows, along irrigation canals, or over marshy areas in open country.

FACING PAGE: High above Big Thompson Canyon, two bighorn rams appear "rimrocked" with no way off a cliff face. Moments later both disappeared over the edge and "pogo-ed" down the precipice to a group of ewes on a ridge below.

RIGHT: A red-naped sapsucker clings to the trunk of an aspen. The birds are regular spring and summer visitors to Colorado.

BELOW: Juvenile male wild turkeys, called "jakes," band together in the spring, perhaps in the hope adult gobblers won't harass them during the breeding season.

Nothing beats dumb luck when photographing wildlife. I had just settled into my blind to photograph pronghorns in the other direction when this white-tailed buck walked between the rising sun and me.

ABOVE: Looking for a way up a rocky chute near Chicago Lakes, I saw one goat, then another, jump across the top. A third one paused at the edge long enough for me to get the camera pointed in the right direction.

FACING PAGE: With the best eyes in the business, this bald eagle seemed to be staring right through me on a bitterly cold winter morning.

RIGHT: Whaddya see? Black-tailed prairie dog youngsters take a look around from the safety of their den in the Pawnee National Grasslands.

BELOW: Leisurely cruising amid the cottonwood seeds on the surface of Watson Lake, a female common merganser, or "fish duck," is likely taking a break from brooding a nearby nest.

The rut is in full swing and a bull elk is leaving his "calling card" by thoroughly thrashing the willows along the stream bank in upper Moraine Park.

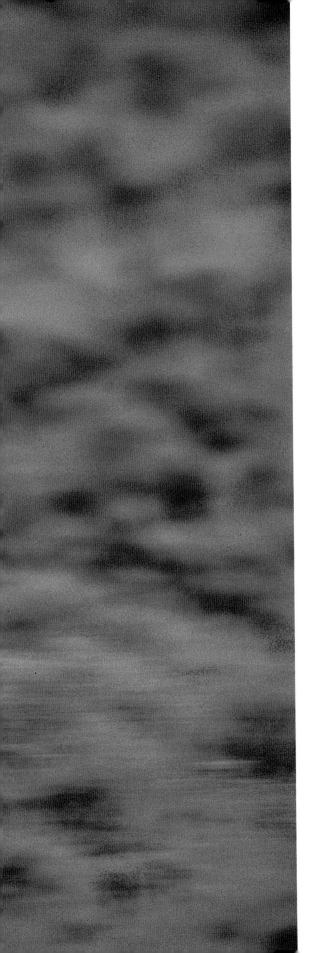

ABOVE: Destined to grow into powerful and efficient night hunters, two great horned owlets are exploring the branches of a nest tree on the South Platte River. They are probably about a month away from flight training.

LEFT: "The only difference between a pronghorn standing still and one going 70 mph is about two steps," a game warden once told me! This buck near Rangely seems to prove that axiom, going from a standing start to full speed in less time than it takes to describe it.

RIGHT: The smallest of three nuthatch species found in Colorado, the pygmy nuthatch neverthe-less shares a few common traits with its cousins: They make use of cavity nests abandoned by the original builders, and they routinely hop headfirst down tree trunks looking for bark-dwelling insects.

BELOW: Male sage grouse gather on strutting grounds, or leks, in April and May to display for and impress the local population of females. The num-ber of males on a given lek varies from fewer than a dozen to more than a hundred.

FAR RIGHT: Amazing senses of hearing, smell, and sight help coyotes locate prey. Here, a young coyote is triangulating a fix on the precise location of a small rodent rustling in the grass, a mouse or vole perhaps. Whatever it is, it is destined to be a snack very soon.

ABOVE: Washing up before dinner? A beaver grooms itself while sitting on the bank of a pond. Colorado's largest rodent, the beaver is a vital member of a healthy riparian ecosystem.

FACING PAGE: Every creature within earshot knows who is in charge of the harem this September morning, as a large bull elk lets out a thunderous bugle.

ABOVE: One of the more beautiful shorebirds, an American avocet, with its long, blue legs and unique, upward-curving beak, casts its reflection on the mirror-like surface of a shallow catch-water puddle in North Park.

LEFT: Although it's a beautiful autumn day, winter can set in at any time at this high-altitude home of the mountain goat. Strong winter winds will keep slopes free of snow, and forage will still be available during the long months ahead.

RIGHT: A fence lizard suns itself on a boulder in Powder Wash in the northwestern part of the state.

BELOW: Although only a few weeks old, these twin mountain goat kids on Mt. Evans can gambol and scramble about on rock ledges and cliff faces that would have human mountaineers whimpering for rope and pitons!

Fattened up, thick necked, and hard antlered, a prime mule deer buck greets a mid-October sunrise in Larimer County. The breeding season is still a few weeks away, but he is already on the prowl.

In failing light, a cow harem trots past a herd bull on an alpine ridge. With the lens focused on the bull, and using a slow shutter speed, the movement of the cows imparts a fantasy-like quality to the scene.

Cute and curious, this yellow-bellied marmot was sound asleep moments earlier in the October sun. In a matter of days, it will crawl into a den under the talus and hibernate for the winter, emerging in May or June to greet the sun's rays once again.

ABOVE: Coyote pups at a den present one of the most difficult photographic tests—getting close enough without mom or dad coyote finding out someone has been there. Special scent-absorbing clothing helped, and much to my delight (and relief) the family remained at the den until the pups were old enough to start hunting.

RIGHT: A pronghorn buck looks out over his domain of sagebrush and high plains in Moffat County.

A great blue heron stretches its neck to study my photo blind on the bank of a farm pond.

ABOVE: As the sun slides under the horizon and another long day of "haying" comes to an end, a little haymaker gives forth a tired yawn before slipping beneath the talus for a well-deserved rest. For a pika, every day of the short alpine summer will be the same—cut, dry, and store winter food—until the cold, deep snows blanket the land.

RIGHT: In spring and fall, lakes and reservoirs in the eastern plains are used by large flocks of migrating snow geese and other waterfowl. It is not unusual in fall for there to be scant few birds one day, then have the water covered by overnight arrivals the next morning, especially just ahead of major weather changes.

FACING PAGE: During the breeding season, bighorn ewes sometimes go to extremes to get away from affectionate rams, but this is a bit ridiculous! This cliff face rises more than 200 feet above the Big Thompson River and the four sheep are about halfway up.

RIGHT: Double-crested cormorants are common summer visitors to some eastern plains and Front Range waters. The bird here was the first one to the roost for the evening. Five more birds landed on the snag by the time the sun dropped below the horizon.

BELOW: The western prairie rattlesnake sometimes gets a bad rap. They aren't aggressive if left alone, but you do have to be on your toes in snake country to avoid inadvertent encounters. In Colorado, rattlesnakes can be found throughout the state, even in some areas up to 9,500 feet in elevation.

A mature bull elk sends forth a challenging bugle on a frosty September morning. For many, it is one of the grandest sounds in the wild.

Stumbling up a dark trail on a tributary of the Cache la Poudre River one September morning, I was startled by the very close crashing sounds of a large animal moving through the forest. My destination was quickly forgotten as the morning light filtered through the trees and the moose bull stepped into this scene.

LEFT: After "remodeling" its new home and having the previous occupants (prairie dogs) for dinner, a badger on the Pawnee Grasslands contemplates its next move. Other prairie dog dens in the area also showed evidence of the badger's handiwork.

BELOW: This coyote slipped in behind me as I examined the old remains of a bighorn ewe on a high alpine ridge in Rocky Mountain National Park. Unconcerned, he remained there until I walked a short distance away, then came down to the bones to perform his own inspection.

A male mountain bluebird alights at a nest cavity with a morsel for the chicks inside. As the chicks grow, both parent birds will make dozens of trips a day to feed them until the youngsters leave the nest in mid-summer.

Soaking up the June sun on the banks of Fall River in Rocky Mountain National Park, this young elk calf is a product of the rut from September past.

RIGHT: A great blue heron huddles, seeming to fortify itself against an icy March day in eastern Colorado.

BELOW: Camouflage doesn't get any better than the changing plumage of a white-tailed ptarmigan. In a couple of weeks, the bird will be completely white except for the beak and eyes. Can you find this one?

Winter has arrived in sheep country, and with it comes the most critical time in the life cycle of mountain wildlife. For these bighorn rams, it may be six months before they taste new, tender green forage. Adequate winter range and minimal disturbance are essential to, but not a guarantee of, survival.

ABOVE: It's summer time and living is about as easy as it gets in the high country. Taking advantage of the abundant food and favorable weather, a young bull elk grows sleek and fat.

RIGHT: As a kid growing up in northern Colorado, I recall that if a Canada goose was seen, it was something people talked about for days. Today, people are still talking about geese, but the tone and content of some of the conversations have changed! The birds have become so common, particularly in some Front Range communities, that geese are considered nuisances in many city parks, on golf courses, and even in some yards.

ABOVE: Early summer mornings and evenings would not be complete without the somber, almost melancholy crooning of mourning doves. The mourning dove is the most widely distributed of the wild doves and pigeons. Spring and fall migrations account for most of the doves in the state, however a few hardy birds are year-round residents.

FACING PAGE: These masked bandits are common throughout Colorado. As opportunistic omnivores, raccoons can be quite bold in their quest for food, and outside pet dishes can be their favorite urban dining spots. Raccoons are generally nocturnal, but this wild pair climbed up on a tree stump in mid-day and made it easy to capture this pleasing portrait. PHOTO BY CHASE SWIFT

ABOVE: This western prairie rattlesnake shakes its tail in an effort to warn intruders to back off. Once you have heard the sound, you'll never forget it!

LEFT: Perhaps the most successful wildlife import to North America, the ring-necked pheasant is found throughout the eastern plains and in some mountain valleys in the state. The crowing of the roosters brightens any early spring day.

A rutting bull elk patrols the perimeter of his cow herd while uttering a hollow, resonant, thumping sound. The noise is not unlike that which can be made by popping your tongue. The cows pay close attention to whatever it means in elk lingo.

Inquisitive, and perhaps a little perplexed, this mountain goat kid has probably never seen a human this close in the middle of winter. Mountain goats are supremely adapted to living at high elevations in alpine and sub-alpine habitats. To survive in these harsh environments, they have thick, dense, wool-like coats and cushion-like inner pads on their hooves. The pads provide for sure-footed traction that is indispensable for living on steep, rocky, and icy slopes. PHOTO BY CHASE SWIFT

Most of the sandhill cranes seen in Colorado are part of the spring and fall migrations. Although rare, some birds may summer in isolated parks and meadows of Jackson, Moffat, and Routt counties in the north-central and northwest regions of the state.

Three mule deer bucks engage in a friendly sparring match on an early-October morning.
In a month or so, however, breeding urges will most likely turn encounters like this into a
decidedly unfriendly, violent skirmish.

ABOVE: A fairly common summer resident of the state, the spotted sandpiper is a small shorebird that bobs up and down in between strides as it searches for food in shallow water and along shorelines.

RIGHT: Certain he hasn't been spotted, a white-tailed jackrabbit remains motionless in a little scratched-out depression called a "form." Technically a hare, the white-tailed variety—in the northern portions of the range—changes color to near white in the winter.

ABOVE: A result of pure luck! When sitting in a blind to photograph waterfowl one fall morning, a flash of red caught my attention. The male northern cardinal was quite curious about the unusual lump—my photo blind—that had appeared sometime during the night near one of his preferred morning perches.

LEFT: A brilliant October pre-dawn glow silhouettes elk on a ridgeline in Horseshoe Park. The unusually rich colors only lasted for a couple of minutes before fading back to softer pastels as the sun rose.

LEFT: Cute, but definitely not cuddly, a young porcupine sleeps soundly on an autumn day. Usually nocturnal, porcupines are found throughout the state and are active year round—except perhaps during the most bitter of cold weather.

FACING PAGE: Hear ye, hear ye. No, this prong-horn buck is not making a speech. Instead, he is perform-ing a lip-curl, which helps his highly complex olfactory system to analyze the scent of female pronghorns (does) for just the right fragrance (pheromones) during the September breeding period.

LEFT: Late September's rich mosaic of shadows, texture, and color engulf the headwaters of Fall River and provide a stunning backdrop for a feeding elk herd. Winter will come to this basin very soon, and it will be left to the winds and snow until June or July.

BELOW: It amazes me that these little puffballs can even fly. The small duck-like divers don't appear to have enough wings or tail to stay airborne! Yet, the pie-billed grebe can fly—though somewhat laboriously and without much grace. It's a good thing they usually land on water, too, as landing is more of a "splashdown" than a controlled descent. Pie-billed grebes are artful underwater swimmers, and they catch their meals below the surface.

LEFT: Even a cold, blustery May drizzle doesn't put a damper on the breeding display of a male blue grouse. A bird of the mountain forests, the blue grouse has a curious "migration" pattern; as winter sets in, the birds move up into the mountains to thick fir and spruce forests.

BELOW: Making this picture also produced one of the more bizarre experiences of my wildlife photography career. While lying on the grassy bank opposite the red fox den, something bumped my boot once, then again. Peering back from under the camouflage ground cover, I was stunned to see an ashen-faced deputy sheriff who thought he had found a body and a crime scene.

FACING PAGE: Partially hidden by rocks, this deer appeared to be a buck, based on body size and conformation; when it raised its head, I was stunned by the monstrous size of this buck!

ABOVE: A summer evening stroll on the shore of a small lake presented this simple yet elegant image. Even in silhouette, the graceful teardrop-shaped bodies, long necks, tall, slender legs, and straight beaks are giveaways to their identity, a pair of black-necked stilts.

FACING PAGE: Hiking across a sagebrush flat one May morning on the way to photograph cottontail rabbits, the antics of a nearby pronghorn doe suggested I might be too close to something. Without moving from the trail, I soon spotted this youngster, perhaps only a day or two old, less than thirty feet away.

LEFT: Having seen the animal from a forest service road, I was nevertheless unprepared when the black bear doubled back on the hillside and appeared in front of me. Moments like these seem to last forever, but there really was only time for one shot before we both went separate directions!

BELOW: As cool fall days warm with the sun, activity on the forest floor is as busy as a downtown sidewalk. All kinds of little critters go about their daily business, which, for this least chipmunk, includes a standing nap in a shaft of sunlight penetrating the canopy.

Early explorers reported the greater prairie chicken "existed in flocks uncountable." This is not the case today. In spring, in places they still inhabit, these residents of native short and tallgrass prairies perform striking courtship dances. On communal display grounds, or leks, the males strut about and stamp their feet, their feathered "horns" (called pinnae feathers) erect and yellow-orange sacs of skin inflated on the sides of the neck, all the while uttering a deep cooing call. They leap and whirl in the air and threaten each other on short runs with tail raised, head down, and "horns" erect. PHOTO BY CHASE SWIFT

LEFT: It's mid-August, and the velvet membrane that has nourished this bull elk's antlers since spring has completed its job. Although it will fall away or be easily rubbed off in a day or so, the impatient bull is trying to help the process along by biting at the dangling strands. His head tossing and tongue work went on for nearly thirty minutes, interrupted only by the stifled laughter of a thoroughly entertained photographer.

BELOW: Diving for dinner—a red fox demonstrates its individual hunting technique. After several launches and nose-first dives, it came up chewing on a mouse or vole. When it looked straight into the lens, it was apparent this hunting style might have some drawbacks; its right eye was gone and completely healed over from an old injury.

ABOVE: An April snowstorm has postponed a wild turkey gobbler's morning dance plans—but only temporarily. As soon as the sun warmed the creek bottom and hens began showing up, the gobbler flew down and commenced to impress the ladies, even though four inches of snow covered the ground.

LEFT: Just as the sun broke over the horizon, a not-too-distant bugle reverberated along the timberline ridge. That prompt, and the urges of the season, spurred this solitary bull elk into a purposeful trot to investigate.

LEFT: Taking a break from nest building, a female red-winged blackbird enjoys a bath in the shallows of her home pond.

BELOW: Had the November sun not reflected off his antler tips, the bedded mule deer buck might have escaped detection in the thick cover of the river bottom. It is the middle of the rut and most likely somewhere in the grass is a bedded doe.

The sandhill crane is one of two crane species native to North America, the other being the critically endangered whooping crane. Standing more than four feet tall when alert, these large, gray birds are sometimes confused with great blue herons. Sandhills are omnivorous and use their stout bills to excavate for worms, snails, frogs, and other morsels. They are also particularly fond of snacking on barley, corn, and wheat in harvested grain fields.

Zeroed in, this springing coyote is about to catch a mouse or vole. The front feet will pin the rodent down—but only long enough for the jaws to snap it up.

Did you hear the one about...? A magpie sits on the neck of a mule deer buck in late winter, looking for ticks and other parasitic insects. The relationship is mutually beneficial— the deer ends up bug free and the magpie gets to eat.

ABOVE: A young red squirrel, also known as "pine squirrel" or "chickaree," has just drunk from a tiny puddle on the top of the rock. Soon it will take its place in the "timber telegraph," chattering announcements of just about everything that moves through its realm.

LEFT: Spring is a time of renewal and rebirth in the mountains. Aspens leaf-out, wildflowers bloom, and newborn elk calves frolic under the watchful eyes of their mothers.

ABOVE: The golden eagle is truly a majestic raptor of open country, whether in the plains, foothills, or mountain regions of the state. While the bald eagle is primarily an angler, the golden eagle is an accomplished hunter. Equipped with incredible talons, a strong hooked beak, and a wingspan approaching seven feet, the golden eagle is perhaps the most imposing bird of prey soaring in Colorado airspace.

FACING PAGE: Fat and fit on a high alpine ridge, a bighorn ram rolls his great horns back for a moments rest. Unlike the antlers of deer or elk, which are renewed annually, the horns of bighorn sheep begin growing at about six months of age and continue to develop throughout their lives. The massive headgear of a large ram may weigh more than twenty-five pounds.

LEFT: Photographing on spring and summer days at small prairie water-holes and ponds is always interesting. You never really know what might show up. At one such pond, I had never before seen a male northern harrier (marsh hawk). Quite a beautiful bird, the male dropped in for a quick bath and left immediately after drying off. Since that day, I have made several visits to the same pond and haven't seen another.

BELOW: Seeing a mountain lion in the wild is an extraordinarily rare occurrence. Actually having a chance to photograph one is the equivalent of winning the lottery. This single image is my only "winning ticket" in more than two decades of wildlife photography.

FACING PAGE: On a snowy November day, it was easy to find a well-used deer trail. Several does had passed earlier, but no buck was with them—very unusual in the middle of the rut. Backtracking the does, I ran smack into this swollen-necked mule deer buck. He paused for only a few moments, then walked around me and continued on down the trail after the does.

In January a few years ago, a bitter Arctic cold front settled on the Front Range. Daytime temperatures hovered around 0 degrees Fahrenheit, and the nights were brutal, in the negative teens and twenties. This scene caught my eye at dusk the evening before, so I went back before daylight the next morning. Sunrise was still a promise when the photo was made, and the little thermometer on my camera pack read -19.

For me, gobbling wild turkeys are a spring equivalent of bugling elk in the fall. The breeding activity—with the thunderous gobbles, tail-fanning struts, and occasional fights between gobblers—is quite similar to the action during the elk rut. The sun was still below the horizon when one of the gobblers in this flock sounded off for the first of many times that day. It was a great day in the field!

ABOVE: A metronome would melt down trying to keep pace with the wing beats of this male rufous hummingbird. While hovering to feed on the narrowleaf penstemon, the little bird's wings are probably cycling about ninety times per second. Due to unique chest and shoulder muscles, hummingbirds are the only birds that can fly backward, sideways, and upside-down. PHOTO BY STEVE VAUGHAN

LEFT: This one is serious! Most bull elk fights don't last very long. Usually, the combatants quickly determine which is the stronger and break off the battle before either gets hurt. That wasn't the case here. For several long minutes, the fight raged and the two bulls tossed each other all over the place. Finally, one of the bulls broke and ran, and the victor punctuated the departure with a vicious antler thrust into the hindquarters of the loser, inflicting what appeared to be fairly grave injuries.

LEFT: Spring is a wonderful time of the year to photograph wildlife, but it can also present identity problems with some of the young subjects. About the size of a tennis ball, this baby rabbit has a bright rusty nape and the inside of the ears are furless, like a desert cottontail. However, the ears appear short and have just a hint of black tipping, like a mountain cottontail. The ranges of the two subspecies overlap in northwestern Colorado where this image was made, so identification is a challenge.

BELOW: Winter is not far away, as the first snowfall of the season piles up on a bedded cow elk and yearling male. Called a "spike," for the shape of his first set of antlers, the young bull's headgear will begin to show the traditional branching of elk antlers in the next set.

LEFT: Six or seven months old, a bighorn lamb is in the midst of perhaps the most critical stage of his young life, his first winter. If conditions are harsh, he may not survive. The very young and the aged are usually the first to succumb to winter's ruthlessness. If he makes it, the horn tips that are just starting to protrude will continue growing for the rest of his life.

FOLLOWING PAGE: Autumn a cappella. When fall rinses vibrant colors into the aspens and morning frosts blanket high meadows, one of the most distinctive and thrilling serenades in the wild reverberates through the mountain air. The bugling of bull elk is a song no wildlife photographer can ignore. Time to go. Hope to see you there.